Gemstones

Beauty, Lore and Fascination

Gemstones
Beauty, Lore and Fascination

By
Michael Babinski

Cover Illustration
by Ed Gedrose

Major Interior Illustrations
by Rebecca Green

INTARSIA PRESS
woodinville, washington.
1995

The Author neither endorses or refutes
any of the beliefs about the supernatural
qualities of gemstones recorded herein.
In any case, medical conditions should
always receive the care and supervision
of a physician.

Table of Contents

Introduction I

A Gem's Journey 3
Physical Characteristics 7
Magical Connotations of Gems ... 11
Synthetics and Imitations 15

The Gemstones 19

Agate 21
Alexandrite 23
Amethyst 25
Aquamarine 29
Diamond 31
Emerald 35
Garnet 37
Iolite 39
Jade 41
Lapis Lazuli 43
Moonstone 45
Opal 47

Pearl 51
Peridot 55
Quartz 57
Ruby 61
Sapphire 63
Tanzanite 65
Topaz 67
Tourmaline 69
Turquoise 71
Zircon 75
Other Gemstones .. 77

Appendix 81

The Birthstones 83
Anniversary Gemstone List 84
Glossary 85
Sources 89

Introduction

The first person to bend down and pick up a glistening pebble of brilliant color must have wondered what made the rock special, why was it so pretty, and what powers might it have. People have been fascinated by gems ever since, asking these same questions time and time again.

Gems have won the hearts of lovers, influenced mighty affairs of state, and provided adornment and decoration throughout history. This book examines some of the folklore and superstitions about gems, and provides a guide to the gemstones you may encounter at your local jeweler.

A Gem's Journey

Gems follow a tortuous path to reach their final place in your jewelry. The route of one such stone, a lovely blue Sapphire, would look much like the following.

Millions of years ago the continental plates in the area that is the Indian ocean collided, producing enormous earthquakes and massive amounts of heat and pressure. This combination caused some of the minerals in the Earth's crust to change and metamorphose into new minerals.

In rare circumstances when a certain mixture of elements were present, the result was a gemstone such as the Sapphire, which crystallized slowly in its extreme environment. At the same time, other types of gems were being formed deep beneath the Earth's crust. In other areas some were formed when volcanic activity pushed molten rock through layers of other minerals on its way to the surface. Then earthquakes created mountains and mountain ranges, bearing the Sapphire up from the depths.

As the mountains eroded with time, rivers cut deep ravines into their sides and exposed the Sapphire, which washed downstream. It collected, along with other heavy stones, in a quiet pool or sandbar along the river's course. The land changed. Rivers disappeared or changed locations, leaving their former courses buried in silt.

Today, local men work all day in a muddy hole in a farmer's field on the island of Sri Lanka. They're digging a dozen feet or so down to one of those accumulations of heavy stones along the course of a long-dead river. In this alluvial deposit they sift through the gravel and find gem pebbles. Most are too poor to bother with, but some will bring them money to feed their families.

A man shows up at the mine once a week or so to sort through their pebbles, some of which are valuable gemstones in the rough. He might make an offer, which they will argue and dicker over until an agreement is reached. Stones in hand, the man travels back to his office in Columbo, the capital city. The next day he visits several cutters who buy parcels of the rough stones which he has collected from many miners. The Sapphire is in one of these lots.

The cutter examines and sorts the stones. He subjects the Sapphire to intense heat in a crude furnace to improve its color, followed by a slow cooling to prevent it from breaking. By doing this, he follows a procedure handed down through generations. He then sorts the gems again, and assigns his workers to cut them.

The Sapphire is fashioned into an oval faceted stone which weighs approximately 2 carats. Separated again for quality and appearance, the stone is included in a parcel of gems sold to another dealer from the USA who specializes in finished stones.

This dealer grades the stones by quality and size again, and heads to the United States. Once there, he calls on a variety of jewelry businesses. There are manufacturers to whom he sells large quantities of the more common commercial-quality stones. The finer material, which is more rare and costly, he saves for the

A Gem's Journey takes many steps from mine to masterpiece

designer goldsmiths who handcraft exquisite jewelry one piece at a time.

The dealer sells the 2 carat Sapphire to a goldsmith in a medium-sized town. The store owner places it on display in her showcase. After a few months, the goldsmith designs a wedding set for a young couple using the Sapphire as the main stone, accented by several small diamonds. They leave the jewelry store with a gemstone which they will cherish throughout their lives. Chances are, in fact, that ten generations from now that blue Sapphire will be gazed upon and admired by their descendants.

Physical Characteristics

There are two main types of gems: Organic and Inorganic.

Organic gems are materials such as amber, pearls, and coral which owe their origin to plants or animals, and whose beauty has inspired people to accept these as gems.

Inorganic gemstones are those minerals and Crystals which possess a gem's essential qualities: beauty, durability, and rarity. These qualities help determine the relative value of each gem species.

Beauty is what attracts us to a mineral and causes it to be worn as ornamentation. A gemstone's beauty may depend on its color, transparency, brilliance, or on a phenomenon such as the play of color exhibited by opal. A gem's desirability may be influenced by the color in demand at the time, proving again that beauty is in the eye of the beholder.

Durability is essential to a gemstone, as it must be able to be worn or used as ornamentation without easily breaking or becoming scratched. There are many minerals, such as purple flourite, which are overlooked as gems because they are very soft or fragile.

Rarity is a valued attribute in gemstones, and adds to the value of specific stones. Gem-quality minerals are just naturally rare, some more than others. How many dull grey rocks do you have to stumble over before you might find one that is brilliant and colorful!

Think of the mountains of minerals, and the relative amounts of gemstone material. Then consider the small percentage of the material which is high enough quality to be cut, sold, and worn.

How is one gemstone different from another? The key factors that make one red stone a Ruby, while another is a Garnet, or perhaps a red Spinel are chemical composition and crystal structure.

Chemical composition describes what makes up a gem. For example, a Diamond is carbon, a Ruby is a compound of aluminum and oxygen, and an Amethyst is silicon and oxygen.

The crystal structure is important too. While diamond and coal are both essentially carbon, the diamond is organized in a crystal form that makes it both hard and beautiful.

These essential attributes also relate to how we choose and value the gems we own.

While you may often consider the relative quality of the gemstone with just a glance, the jeweler evaluates quality with precision instruments and a practiced eye. Several factors must be considered.

Transparency: Should this gem be transparent, translucent, or opaque? Is it cut in a fashion which shows off the material to its best advantage and potential?

Color: The color of the gem should appeal to you, that is the most important thing. The jeweler will assess the quality of the color in several ways:

Hue – Just what color is it? Red, blue, green…
or is it a pinkish red, yellowish green and so on.
Saturation – This is the intensity and amount
of the color present. Stones with high saturation are vivid and electric in their color, while
gems lacking in saturation will appear grayish
or brownish.
Tone – The relative lightness or darkness of a
stone. Some aquamarines, for instance, barely
have a hint of blue to distinguish them from
colorless, while some sapphires have so much
blue in them so as to appear black. A good
gemstone has a tone which falls into a pleasing
range and allows the hue and saturation to be
seen.

Clarity: Virtually all gemstones have some inclusions ranging from microscopic specks to those which
render the stone opaque. An inclusion, commonly
called a flaw, is a bit of material or a characteristic
captured within a mineral gemstone's body during its
formation. This could be a stress fracture or a bit of
another gem.

Some gem types tend to have more inclusions than
others. Emerald, for example, almost always has inclusions that are visible to the naked eye, while blue Topaz
rarely does. Because of the varying amounts of inclusions different gemstone species tend to have, they are
accordingly judged by different standards.

Generally, the fewer the inclusions, the higher the
gem's quality. We might, however, accept an Emerald

with many inclusions because of the overall beauty and fine color of the individual stone, while a blue Topaz with the same amount of inclusions would be rejected.

In addition to a gemstone's quality and appearance, there is the criterion of wearability. As you look through the sections on each gem in this book, you will see ratings for toughness and hardness.

Toughness is a gem's resistance to breakage. Although a stone may be exceptionally hard, it might still be breakable. A diamond can be broken with a sharp hammer blow, even though it is the hardest thing on earth.

Hardness is the resistance to scratching and is commonly measured on a comparison basis which is called the Moh's hardness scale. It rates the different minerals by which will scratch which. The higher a gem's number on the scale of 1-10, the more it will scratch and the fewer will scratch it. It is important to note, however, that the differences between the numbers on the scale are not equal. For example, Diamond at 10 on the scale is approximately 140 times harder than Corundum (Ruby and Sapphire) which measures a 9 on the scale. However, Corundum is only about twice as hard as Topaz, which is 8 on the scale.

You will want to think about the type of wear or use you might put a gemstone to, and choose one with appropriate hardness and toughness to be suitable.

Magical Connotations of Gems

Since the dawn of history, gems have shared a value as ornament with their place as amulets, talismans, and charms.

In early Roman times, a scholar by the name of Pliny wrote an encyclopedic work entitled "Natural History" which, along with observations on a wide variety of subjects, compiled many then-contemporary beliefs on the powers of gemstones. From that time until the Middle Ages, philosophers and mystics wrote books called "Lapidaries" which expounded on the magical properties of gemstones – their powers to heal, predict, protect, and change the course of human affairs.

How did these beliefs arise in the first place? As humans looked at the world around them, they saw that certain objects' beauty made them stand out from the rest. Among the dull grey rocks were some that sparkled and scintillated with dazzling color. These were thought to be of a higher nature, i.e. closer to God, more akin to the supernatural than related to the baser earth. Some legends call for gemstones being descended from heaven, or formed by lightning.

The stone's color often determined its associations. Red stones were related to blood, blue stones to the sky, yellow stones to the sun. Bright hot colors like red were linked to activity, courage and vigor, while cooler colors like green and blue were thought to emphasize the calmer, more contemplative aspects of humankind.

Sometimes the form or physical characteristics made the connection. Moonstone and pearl were both linked to the moon because of their resemblances to it.

The gem's potential could be further increased by fashioning it into an amulet. The gem crystal's natural power was augmented by the spirit and craftsmanship of an artisan's work. Sometimes the talisman was adorned with mystical symbols or runes, either carved into the stone or worked in a metal design around it. Combinations of gemstones were sometimes prescribed to yield certain effects. In some cultures the gem was powdered and swallowed to release its healing properties.

Even today, beliefs about the powers of gemstones persist both in developing countries and in the heart of the modern industrialized world. People often wear their birthstone or those of their mate or children, a practise rooted in mysticism, but accepted by custom of tradition. The New Age movement has taken up wearing uncut crystals and demonstrates a rebirth of interest in gems' spiritual powers. The old established Churches still have their jewelled altar ornaments and bishop's rings.

After all, what was called magic in the old days, we know as science today. The study of the stars which was Astrology evolved into Astronomy, and the chemical explorations of Alchemy spawned the modern science of Chemistry. You might say that as we gained more knowledge about our universe, we perfected our magic, and started calling it by a new name – science.

Today, legitimate scientists study subjects like telekinesis, telepathy and quantum physics. What are these but fancy names for magic? In fact, there are some gemstones which will readily demonstrate "magical" powers. Tourmaline will produce a charge of static electricity when warmed, and will attract dust and fluff: we call this pyroelectricity. Quartz generates electricity when put under pressure or stress, and will vibrate when electricity is applied to the stone. This is called piezoelectricity and makes modern Quartz watches work.

The Ancients thought gems acted as lenses to focus some underlying field or power, or to release a human potential. Our science may someday reveal whether this is truth or fanciful speculation.

Are gemstones' legendary powers real? When the warrior who wore a gem into battle returned triumphant, he gave credit for his victory to the gem's powers. It could be that wearing the gem and believing in it's protection gave him a bit more confidence and assurance, and that kept him unharmed. Or maybe the gem did exert an influence. Not much, but just enough to sway luck and turn aside a sword's blow by a few inches. Perhaps in the end it was just coincidence.

Who's to say? In our modern rational world we believe in science and so it works for us. In the old times, they believed in magic and thought it worked for them. It is only when you realize that you don't have all the answers that you can begin to pursue wisdom.

Synthetics And Imitations

Almost as long as people have known gemstones, we've tried to imitate their beauty. The ancient Egyptians made a blue ceramic called Faience, and eventually developed glass to imitate Turquoise and Lapis Lazuli. Later cultures followed in this tradition and developed it into a varied and precise art. Today, synthetic and imitation stones are produced in laboratories by complex technologies.

A few definitions in terms about gemstones are worth mentioning here.

Natural Gemstones are taken from nature, dug from the ground or produced organically, and has only been cut and polished.

Genuine Gemstones are natural gemstones which have been enhanced using one or more methods. Examples include heating a Ruby to intensify the color, irradiating a Topaz to produce the blue color, using colorless oil to mask inclusions in an Emerald, and so on. Since these enhancements are common and durable, many are accepted as trade practices. Chances are you may never have seen an unheated Ruby or Sapphire. Certain other enhancements such as dyeing, or filling cracks in gems with glass, are not considered normal and acceptable. For more information, ask your jeweler about enhancements.

Synthetic Stones are exact chemical and crystal replicas, made in laboratories, of natural gemstones. Various types may differ in price, from very cheap to hundreds of dollars per carat. This is because some synthetics are produced by more costly and difficult methods which more closely replicate nature. All synthetic stones lack rarity, however, because laboratories can produce them in whatever quantity is desired.

Imitation Stones are those which merely try to look like a genuine gemstone. Examples of imitations include glass or plastic used to imitate sapphire or aquamarine, synthetic sapphire which is treated to imitate alexandrite, and stones like howlite dyed blue to imitate turquoise.

How does the jeweler tell which is the genuine article? In Pliny's "Natural History" he described ways to distinguish genuine stones from frauds. He said to check the weight and coldness, since he asserted that natural stones were both heavier and felt colder to the touch than imitations. He also recommended checking for bubbles within the stone, a rough finish, and dull lusterless appearance.

Modern gemologists use an array of scientific tests to verify a gem's proper classification. These may include measuring a gem's refraction to determine the amount the stone bends light, and checking to see if the stone is singly or doubly refractive, that is, whether it splits the light which passes through it. They may also consult a spectroscope to determine what wavelengths of light the stone absorbs. They will usually examine the stone under magnification to identify key inclusions inside it. By combining the clues from several tests, and matching the results to known data about gemstones, the stone's true identity is revealed.

The Gemstones

Agate

"She is the fairies midwife, and she comes
In shape no bigger than an agate stone
On the forefinger of an alderman"
William Shakespeare,
Romeo and Juliet Act 1, scene 5

Also known as Chalcedony, Agate's many subspecies are distinguished by their colors and patterns. Tiny crystals of Quartz interlock to form Agate, which is always opaque to translucent because of this. Some types of Agate are:

Carnelian: Yellow-orange to orangey red, translucent. Credited with turning away the evil eye, strengthening the spirit, and protecting from misfortune. Carnelian was also thought to give courage to the timid, banish sadness, encourage friendships and bring contentment.

Chrysocolla: Intense light blue or blue-green Agate containing the mineral Chrysocolla.

Chrysoprase: Light to medium yellowish green, translucent. Was once considered to be a prized form of Jade.

Bloodstone: Dark green with dark red spots, opaque. Legends say that Bloodstone was formed from drops of Christ's blood as he was crucified. It was thought to have the power to stop bleeding, give wisdom, and protect against enemies.

Blue Lace Agate: Lavender to light blue with lacy white lines, translucent. Supposed to aid in contemplation and meditation.

Fire Agate: Iridescent colors against a brown body color, translucent.

Jasper: Differing opaque colors, usually green red or yellow. Also picture Jasper showing landscape like patterns. Jasper had the attribute of bringing rain to drought ridden lands, and of curing epilepsy and cancer.

Moss Agate: Brown or green inclusions that look like moss or leaves, translucent. A helpful talisman for the gardener, to ensure that plants would grow healthy and strong.

Onyx or Sardonyx: Banded or solid color opaque Agate. Offered protection from the evil eye and empowered the mind and spirit. Also reputed to bring sexual bliss, and monetary success to its owner, if it was worn at all times by its owner.

Petrified Wood: Wood that has been replaced by Agate which follows the wood's structure.

Agate in general was thought to protect and give courage to its wearer, and to help against bad dreams and insomnia. Some sources credit Agate with preventing skin ailments and cooling fevers. It is known in the Middle East that an Agate pebble held in the mouth will relieve thirst.

Hardness: 6.5-7
Toughness: Good

Alexandrite

Alexandrite is a rare form of the gemstone chrysoberyl, and changes color in different lighting. In daylight or florescent lighting it shows a bluish green or yellowish green color, whereas in incandescent light it appears brownish red or purplish red. The finest examples show a strong color change from a true green to a vibrant red. Attractive, fine quality Alexandrites are very scarce and command a high price. Today Alexandrite is found in Brazil and Sri Lanka, although it was first mined in Russia.

The name Alexandrite was given to the gem because its first discovery in Russia's Ural mountains coincided with the birthday of Alexander II, who later became Czar. This was considered a good omen, and the stone acquired a reputation as a good luck amulet. The red and green colors exhibited by the gem also were the same as the colors worn by the czarist military. These factors, combined with its rarity and unusual nature, made Alexandrite a favorite among the Russian aristocracy. Many of the finest examples of Alexandrite exist in old estate jewelry, although the stone has been widely imitated.

Hardness: 8.5
Toughness: Excellent
Birthstone: June (along with Pearl)

Necklace with Citrine, Black Jade and Diamonds in
14 Karat Gold, With Baroque Pearls.

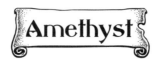

Amethyst

Often found in the form of six sided crystals, Amethyst is a purple form of Quartz mined primarily in South America and Africa. Its rich coloration, good durability, and relative affordability make Amethyst a popular choice for all types of jewelry.

Amethyst is a stone that was well known to the Ancients, being at the time more highly prized than many gems which today enjoy more recognition and value, including Sapphire and Ruby.

The rich purple gemstone enjoys a wealth of legends and folklore from throughout history. The ancient Greek word Amethystos, from whence the name amethyst arises, means 'without wine.' The stone was thought to be an amulet against excessive drunkenness. Later legends say that a goblet or cup fashioned entirely from Amethyst allows the drinker to consume wine from it without feeling intoxicated.

Amethyst was known as a gem which would bring forth the highest, purest aspirations of humankind. Chastity, sobriety, and the control over one's thoughts were all attributes heightened by wearing Amethyst. The gem would guard against the anger of passion, and the violent or base nature of its wearer. Instead the stone encouraged calm, bravery and contemplation.

One legend says that the gemstone comes from the beautiful maiden Amethyst, a devotee of the goddess Diana. Diana turned the girl to clear stone to protect her from tigers conjured up by an angry Bacchus, the Greek god of wine. When Bacchus saw what he had caused, he was remorseful and poured his wine over the stone, staining it purple.

Amethyst has had its place in the Christian church, worn on Bishops' rings, the royal purple color used to symbolize Christ. Saint Valentine was thought to wear a ring set with an antique Amethyst carved with an image of Cupid. The stone also is a symbol of Saint Matthias.

Hardness: 7
Toughness: Good
Birthstone: February

Amethyst's purple color caused it to be associated with wine.

Aquamarine was thought to protect sailors and their ships.

Aquamarine

The very name, Aquamarine, comes from a Latin word for seawater. With its light greenish blue hue, the gemstone lives up to it's nomenclature. Most commonly cut as a faceted stone, the color and clear brilliance of the gem make it a true beauty.

Occasionally Aquamarine is found in large enough pieces to yield finished gemstones into the 1000-plus carat range, although most gem quality stones that are used for jewelry are much smaller. Because of its color and name, Aquamarine, a form of the mineral Beryl, has always been a favorite of seafaring folk. It was believed to ensure safe and prosperous voyages upon the sea, and to guard against storms.

This gemstone is found primarily in Brazil, Nigeria, and Afghanistan, and is usually heat treated to purify the blue and remove excessive green tones. While being Beryl makes it kin to Emerald, Aquamarine is usually free from major inclusions.

There are many qualities attributed to Aquamarine in folkloric circles. It was thought to be the symbol of happiness and everlasting youth, to bring victory in battle and in legal disputes, and to re-awaken love in long-married couples.

The Gem was credited with curing belching and yawning, and for being especially effective at warding off ailments of the jaws, throat, stomach and liver. It was believed to protect against poisoning and relieve toothaches. People have used Aquamarine in ceremonies in the belief that it would bring rain when needed, or visit drought upon their enemies.

Aquamarine's color was also thought to be symbolic of the moon. When worn as an amulet, it was reputed to bring relief of pain and to make the wearer more friendly, quicken the intellect, and cure laziness. Cut as a crystal ball, Aquamarine was thought to be a superior stone for crystal gazing and fortune telling.

Hardness: 7.5-8
Toughness: Good
Birthstone: March

Diamond

Neither the rarest nor most expensive of gemstones, Diamond is nevertheless the most celebrated. Why then mankind's long-held fascination with this usually near colorless stone?

Diamond is hard. Ten on the Moh's scale of 1-10, Diamond is approximately 140 times harder than any other mineral. The supreme hardness means that Diamond, while it can be shattered, cannot be scratched by anything other than another diamond. This hardness caused the ancient Greeks to name the stone "Adamas," which means invincible. Later this evolved into the word diamond.

Diamond is distintive in the way it reflects light. It has a unique brilliance and also breaks the light up into spectral colors which dance within the stone as it is moved. Another unusual quality of a Diamond is its purity. A gem quality diamond is among the purest elements found in nature.

So, just what is Diamond? It is the element carbon, crystallized in an inimitable molecular structure that makes it so hard and beautiful. Diamond has a crystal form in the cubic system, and most often occurs as an octahedron shape. An octahedron is like a pair of four sided, pyramids placed together base to base. The wizard on the cover of this book holds an octahedron shaped crystal.

Diamonds actually occur in all different colors, true red being most rare, followed by blue. Diamonds formed deep within the earth where the pressure and heat are intense.

Volcanic activity eons ago brought diamond to the surface where it is found today in either the original volcanic rock formations or where it has weathered out and washed away from them. The cores of ancient volcanos that hold diamonds are composed of a mineral called Kimberlite and occur in many areas of the world. Diamond mining is quite a job. For each one carat Diamond, an average of 260 tons of ground must be moved.

The principle producers of Diamonds today are Australia, the Soviet Union, and several different nations in southern Africa. Diamonds, though, are found in small quantities in many places, even the USA.

Because of its unusual qualities Diamond occupies a powerful place in folklore. It was not until the 16th century that Diamond was first able to be cut and polished, thereby yielding it's true beauty. Still, the Ancient Greeks wore Diamonds into battle on their shields believing the stones could lend them their invincibility.

In Medieval times, uncut octahedron Diamond crystals were often set into rings, and their exposed points earned these rings the name "Glass Cutter Rings." Diamond was believed to symbolize purity and innocence, and a joyful life of faith and piety. It also offered the ability to detect poison, as its surface was said to cloud in the toxin's presence.

The Ancients knew Diamond as the king of gems, and credited it with strong powers to ward off evil, protect people from lightning, and give courage to soldiers in battle. They thought that the only way to break the gem was to first steep it in goat's blood.

The tale is told of how early Diamond merchants from Europe sometimes took advantage of the locals' in India, an early source of Diamonds. They would smash the local miner's large Diamond with a hammer thus "proving" it not to be a true Diamond, then return later to collect the remaining pieces from which smaller gems could still be cut.

Today, Diamonds are widely thought of as a symbol of romantic love, prized since the Duke of Burgundy's time as the stone of choice for engagement rings. The Gemstone's durability and resistance to wear has also led to the saying "a Diamond is forever."

Hardness: 10
Toughness: Excellent
Birthstone: April

Ladies' Diamond Ring; 14 Karat Gold.

Emerald

This rich green form of the mineral Beryl gets its name from the Latin and Greek term 'Smaragdus.' Even fine examples often show inclusions, while poorer stones may be completely opaque.

The inclusions cause Emerald to be somewhat on the fragile side. Thought should be given to designing jewelry which protects the stone from harsh wear. As part of the normal fashioning process, most Emeralds are immersed in clear oil to fill minute voids. Emerald is found today primarily in Columbia, Brazil, Zambia, and Zimbabwe, though it has a rich history stretching into ancient times.

The first known Emerald mines were in southern Egypt and show evidence of being worked since 2000 BC. The ancient Egyptians believed Emerald stood for fertility and rebirth.

The stone also was prized in ancient Rome, where many Roman citizens wore Emerald jewelry, some of which has survived to this day. Nero supposedly viewed the gladiators' fights through a lens cut from a large transparent emerald because he found the color calming.

In some legends of King Arthur, the Holy Grail is described as being fashioned from an Emerald. Stories also say that a serpent which gazes upon Emerald is immediately blinded.

Emerald was used in the Middle Ages to foretell the future, and was thought to ward off evil sorcery and cure demonic possession. It was also believed to be a symbol of faith and loyal friendship. The gem was closely associated with love, and with contentment in marriage. Its calming, healing nature in legends is evidentially a result of its soothing color. As such it was thought to be good for eye ailments and irritations.

Emeralds were among the treasures brought back by the conquistadors from the new world. Treasure hunters have found gold ornaments set with Emeralds on sunken galleons. Early stone cutters kept an Emerald on their workbench so as to rest their eyes with a gaze at its soothing color.

The Emerald's use in ancient medicines was wide-spread and Emerald was thought to cure a wide range of ills, from poor eyesight to infertility. It was believed to ease childbirth, and aid the liver, as well as guard against fits and convulsions. Even today, the powder of poorer quality Emeralds is used in folk medicines in China.

Hardness: 7.5-8
Toughness: Varies poor to good
Birthstone: May

Garnet

Most people think of Garnet as a single type of stone that is dark red, but actually Garnet is a family of gems that spans a range of colors. Some of these are:

Almandite Garnet: Reddish orange to red.

Andradite Garnet: Yellow, green, brown, or black.

Grossularite Garnet: Green, yellow. Green Grossularite, also known as Tsavorite, comes from Kenya's Tsavo region.

Malaya Garnet: Slightly pinkish orange or reddish orange.

Hydrogrossular Garnet: Translucent green, closely resembles Nephrite Jade.

Pyrope Garnet: Medium to dark red.

Rhodolite Garnet: Light to dark pink to purplish red.

Spessartite Garnet: Yellowish orange to reddish orange.

These stones all share the name Garnet which comes from the Latin 'Granatus' which means "seedlike." Many Garnet crystals have the shape and color of pomegranate seeds. In ancient times it was known as Carbuncle which relates to the color and refers to a boil or blister. (The name Carbuncle was also applied to other red gems, but especially to red Garnet.)

Garnet has been believed to cure heart palpitations, lung diseases, and diseases of the blood. It was thought to represent faith, consistency, and truth. Garnets were claimed to help the wearer resist melancholy and warn off evil spirits, especially spirits of the night. The gemstone was endowed with the power to protect against poison, and was believed to inspire contemplation and induce a joyous state. It was also a stone of loyalty and truthfulness, and offered its wearer the power to protect their standing and possessions.

Today, Garnet is found in many locations and is principally supplied from Africa, North America, and India.

Hardness: 7-7.5
Toughness: Fair to good
Birthstone: January

Iolite

The name for Iolite is taken from the root of the word violet. Appropriately enough, Iolite is a slightly purplish blue—really a dark violet color. Iolite is dichroic (it has also been called Dichroite), so from different directions it may also show light brown or even colorless. It is the blue to colorless shift which earned it the old misnomer 'water sapphire.'

Iolite is commonly cut in faceted shapes, while the more translucent stones are fashioned into cabochons or carvings for signet rings. This gem is primarily found in India, Tanzania, and Sri Lanka and is used to commemorate the 21st wedding anniversary. Friendliness and higher, purer thoughts were ascribed to Iolite's influences. It was thought to promote charity and helpfulness. Legends describe Iolite as strengthening eyesight.

In ancient times Viking mariners used a thin slice of Iolite to help in navigation. Because its strong dichroism makes it act like polarized sunglasses, its properties helped the Vikings locate the true position of the sun on cloudy or hazy days.

Hardness: 7-7.5
Toughness: Fair

Ladies' Iolite Ring, 14 Karat Gold.

Jade

Two types of stones can rightly claim the name Jade: Nephrite Jade and Jadeite. Nephrite occurs in light- to dark-green, yellow to brown, and in white, gray or black. It is primarily found in Taiwan, Canada, Australia, and New Zealand.

It was used by the ancient South American cultures in ornamental objects and as axheads. In fact, the ancient Mexican hieroglyph for precious stone refers primarily to Jade. Jade stones representing the heart were placed in the sarcophagi of the dead. Maori tribes in New Zealand fashioned their legendary war clubs and ceremonial carvings from Nephrite.

Jadeite is found in the same colors as Nephrite, plus red and lavender. The green of Jadeite is more lively and the most even, intense green Jadeite which is semi-transparent is known as Imperial Jade. It is found in Burma.

Because of the way that Jade's microscopic crystals link together, it is exceptionally tough and resists breakage like no other stone.

Jade was used extensively in daily and ceremonial objects of Chinese nobility, and represented high rank and authority. It was commonly carved into meaningful shapes such as fish, birds, bats, or dragons. The Chinese believed that since Jade objects lasted so long, due no doubt to Jade's toughness, that Jade was linked to immortality. Jade amulets were also buried with the dead in China. Symbolic circles called "pi," which represent infinity, were carved of the gemstone. In Taoism, the supreme heavenly god is called the "Jade Emperor." The Chinese still revere Jade and believe that it brings good luck, benevolence, purity, and enhanced intelligence.

Legends about Jade include a wide range of healing influences – of the eyes, nervous system and of the organs, particularly the kidneys. It was worn in amulets over the kidney area, and on the arm, and was reputed to magically effect the removal of kidney stones.

Hardness
    Jadeite: 6.5-7
    Nephrite: 6-6.5
Toughness: Exceptional

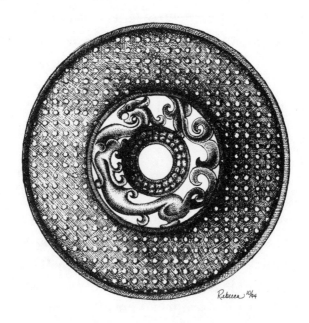

Rebecca 10/94

Lapis Lazuli

Found in Afghanistan and Chile, Lapis Lazuli was well known to the Egyptian pharaohs and in Persian kingdoms. It was highly valued due to its relative scarcity and was used in Tutankhamun's famous burial mask. The ancient Egyptians regarded the stone as a symbol of the heavens, and wore it carved in designs representing various deities and religious images. Faience, an ancient Egyptian pottery, was made to imitate Lapis Lazuli and turquoise for the masses.

Lapis Lazuli is a vivid blue opaque gemstone that is a composite of several minerals including Lazurite, Calcite, and Sodalite. It is generally a mottled blue color. Frequent inclusions of pyrite may pepper the stone with golden colored spangles. Its name comes from the Latin word 'Lapis' meaning stone and an Arabic word 'Azul' meaning blue. It was also used in European cultures to symbolize the heavens in which the stars are held, and in some cultures to signify chastity. Lapis Lazuli was thought to be a cure for melancholy and fever.

Some people believed that the ten commandments were in fact carved on tablets of Lapis Lazuli. Legends describe Lapis Lazuli as being a favorite stone of the alchemists. It was thought to bestow wisdom and promote truth. By placing it on a painful area or where swelling occurred, it was thought to provide relief. The gemstone was worn as a talisman to attract friends, gain favors, and protect the wearer in darkness. In times past it was ground to produce the pigment ultramarine, although this color is now synthesized.

Hardness: 5-6
Toughness: Fair

Moonstone

Moonstone is a type of feldspar which shimmers with an elusive glow when a light is shined upon it. Caused by tiny albite inclusions which reflect and scatter light, this effect mimics the moon's soft glow, hence the gem's name. It is most often white but also occurs as softly tinted colors of peach, grey, and green.

Many of this gem's legends come from its association with the moon. The ancient Greeks and Romans linked the stone with moon deities, most often representing the feminine side of creation. It was thought to be an important gift when given to a lover, and would allow one to tell the future if held in the mouth during a full moon. A Moonstone placed beneath the pillow or worn while sleeping induced dreams that prophesied the future.

Pope Leo X was said to have a Moonstone that undertook a visible change in character in tune with the phases of the moon. Other European tales tell of how moonstone had the power to cure fever, arouse passion, and protect from moonstroke and lunacy. It was also believed to ward off cancer and protect the traveler.

Owing perhaps to the fact that Moonstone is primarily found in India, Sri Lanka, and Burma, many Indian legends surround the gem. Hindu legends hold that Moonstone was actually solidified moonbeams which reached earth, and revere it as a good luck object. Indian astrologers use Moonstone to befriend the moon and make use of its energy.

Set as a talisman, or powdered and boiled with lemon juice and other extracts, Moonstone is credited with curing anxiety, strengthening resolve, and relieving high blood pressure.

Hardness: 6 - 6.5
Toughness: Poor
Second Alternate birthstone for June

Moonstone evokes the moon's elusive glow.

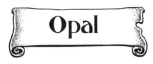

Opal

Opal is a gemstone that ranges from semi-transparent to opaque. Opal's body color covers a broad spectrum of colors, but it is mostly prized for what is known as 'play of color.' This is the ability to reflect and break up light into multiple colors which occur as medium- to broad-sized pinpoints, or larger flashes within the stone. Play of color occurs in only a fraction of Opal stones, and the rest of the non-precious opal is known as potch.

Opal was formed when silica was liquefied and washed down into fissures in the surrounding rock, where it then solidified into a hardened gel. Unlike most other gemstones, Opal is therefore not a crystal, but rather an amorphous solid. Microscopic silica spheres sometimes would line up in a pattern which acts as a diffraction grating, which has a prism like effect and produces the brilliant plays of color.

Opal today is mostly found in Australia, Mexico, and the USA. Its name comes from the Sanskrit "Upala" and the later Greek derivative "Opallios," meaning to see a change of color. There are several types of naturally occurring opals:

White Opal: A transparent or white body color with play of color.

Black Opal: Blue, grey, or black body color sets off the play of color.

Fire Opal: Yellow to orange body color; may have play of color or if not, is often fashioned into faceted stones.

Boulder Opal: Most often black Opal which has occurred in thin veins; the resulting cut stones have a layer of Opal with some of the ironstone matrix still intact.

In addition to these completely natural stones, stonecutters create some assembled Opal gemstones:

Opal Doublet: A thin slice of Opal is glued to a black or brown backing stone to enhance its color and makes it durable enough for wear.

Opal Triplet: Same as an Opal doublet, but with a clear quartz or glass cap added on top of the Opal for added durability. The slice of Opal used in the triplet is often much thinner.

The ancient Romans called Opal the queen of gems because it encompassed the colors of all the other gems. They revered Opal as a symbol of hope and purity and held it to be second only to the prized Emerald. At that time Opal, called by the Latin "Opalus," was primarily found in India.

In later times, women in Scandinavian countries wore opals as hair ornaments in the belief that it preserved their blond hair and kept it from going grey.

The Arabs thought that opals were formed by lightning strikes and that this is why the brilliant flashes of color are captured within. Other legends said that Opal would act to ward off lightning, and give the cloak of invisibility to its wearer when desired. It was supposed to grant vigor, aid the heart and kidneys, and protect against fainting and infection.

A modern folktale, in which a person should not wear Opal unless it is either their birthstone or a gift, traces its roots to the 1817 novel by Sir Walter Scott, "Anne of Geierstein," in which Opal is associated with misfortune borne by the heroine.

Opal should be treated with some care to prevent sharp blows, scratches, and should never be kept in oil or other chemicals. Opal contains a percentage of water as part of the stone; it need not be kept in water, but should never be stored in a bank vault for long periods of time because of the dehumidifiers used in many vaults.

Hardness: 5-6.5
Toughness: poor to fair
Birthstone: October (along with pink tourmaline)

Pearl

A Pearl is formed when, in response to an irritant within their shell, certain types of mollusks secrete nacre and build up a smooth coating around the irritating object. With cultured pearls, the irritant is provided by man, but in natural pearls, this irritant is most likely a parasite or grain of sand. Cultured pearls are most prevalent today, but only from the 20th century on. Many layers of nacre, which is composed of tiny interlocked crystals of aragonite, form a Pearl.

Although many mollusks form pearls, we value those with 'lustre,' a soft sheen of reflected light which is formed only by certain mollusk species, specifically oysters. Pearls are most commonly thought of as white, but many colors abound such as cream, pink-peach, blue-grey, and black.

There are two main types of pearls: Saltwater and Freshwater.

Saltwater Cultured Pearls are produced when the oyster is implanted with a round Mother of Pearl sphere cut from a Mississippi river clam shell. The Pearl that results is either round, or freeform based on round, or anything in between. Saltwater Pearls are primarily Akoya pearls from Japan, which range in size up to 10-12mm, and the South Seas pearls which are generally much larger and include the prized natural color black pearls. In the past, natural pearls were predominantly found in Ceylon, Scotland and Norway, and especially the Persian Gulf.

Freshwater Cultured Pearls are produced by different varieties of freshwater clams, and get their start from a bit of another type of mollusk's flesh implanted within the host creature. The result are pearls with freeform, often fantastic shapes. The most well known freshwater Pearls come from Lake Biwa, Japan and from certain rivers in China. American rivers produce freshwater Pearls, and culturing these in the Mississippi has begun to yield Pearls in usable quantities.

Pearls were among the treasures sent to Europe by the Conquistadors, but overfishing of the pearl beds by the Spanish invaders caused depletion of the mollusks, ending the harvest.

Pearls have long been used in Asian medicine, and are thought to be efficacious in the cure of eye ailments, heart trouble, indigestion, fever and bleeding. They are sometimes taken like pills or ground up as medicine components. Since pearls are in fact rich in calcium, they actually would be very effective in aiding indigestion and curing heartburn.

The Chinese have a legend that pearls fall to the earth as rain when dragons fight in the sky, and that pearls offer protection against fire breathing dragons.

Western beliefs held that pearls could cure mental illness and soothe heartbreak for the wearer. They were also credited with being a powerful antidote against poison. Ancient tales tell of how rain, or the tears of angels, was supposed to have fallen in the open shells of oysters, which turned the drops to Pearls. When manna fell from Heaven, it was believed to have been accompanied by Pearls and precious gems. Pearls were symbolic of purity and clarity, and were associated with the moon. Moslem writings refer to the "Pearl of Paradise" and it is said that heaven is beautified by many red Pearls.

Cleopatra was said to have dissolved a pearl in wine and swallowed it to seduce Mark Antony. The Pearl was thought to be a powerful aphrodisiac, and to attract love.

One of the most ardent admirers of pearls was Queen Elizabeth I of England, who wore dresses studded with pearls of incredible richness. She was reputed to have confiscated several fine Pearl necklaces from Mary, Queen of Scots. Still pearls were favorites of many other European royal figures. Henry VIII wore a massive gold crown studded with rubies, sapphires, diamonds, and 19 pearls, as well as a necklace set with large round pearls. Rudolph II, emperor of the Holy Roman Empire, was fond of pearls and collected pearls from America.

Hardness: 2.5-4.5
Toughness: Variable
Birthstone: June (along with Alexandrite)

Peridot

Peridot is a transparent to translucent gem that ranges in color from light yellowish green to a deep olive green color, and is usually faceted or sometimes cabochon cut.

Peridot gets its name from an Arabic word "faridat" meaning 'gem.' It was also sometimes known as Olivine. In olden times, Peridot was often confused with topaz or emerald. The ancient Egyptians knew it as the gem of the sun, and mined it on an island in the Red Sea, just off Egypt's coast.

To develop it's full potential as a talisman, it was thought that Peridot must be set in yellow Gold. It would then protect its wearer against nightmares and terrors of the night, and served to ward off the evil eye.

Other legends credit Peridot with bringing happiness and good cheer, attracting lovers, and strengthening the eyes. It was also said to aid in digestion, and to cure liver ailments.

If strung on a Jackass' hair and worn tied to the left arm, Peridot would keep evil spirits at bay. Pliny wrote that Peridot was dull during daylight hours, but would glow like a hot coal by night.

Peridot is found today mostly in the USA, but also Australia, Brazil, and Burma. Care should be taken to protect Peridot from rough treatment and sudden temperature changes.

Hardness: 6.5-7
Toughness: Fair to good
Birthstone: August

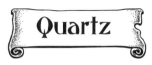

Quartz

The most famous Quartz is of course Amethyst (see separate heading), but in fact there are many forms of this gemstone:

Here are a few

Citrine: A transparent form of Quartz that varies from light yellow through deep orange in color. Found mostly in Brazil, Bolivia, and Spain, Citrine is usually heated to improve its color. Not to be confused with Topaz. Citrine was thought to bring a calm, objective attitude, and make its wearer cheerful.

Rock Crystal: Clear transparent Quartz, often used as pointed natural crystals or cut into carvings or crystal balls. This form of Quartz was used in ceremonies by Native Americans, and is sometimes carried in the Shaman's medicine bag. The Japanese are said to be fond of the Rock Crystal ball as an instrument of contemplation.

Rose Quartz: Translucent light to medium pink gemstone: can occur as a star stone. Rose Quartz was reputed to have a calming effect, heightening feelings of creativity and peacefulness. It is the gem from which the lenses of rose-colored glasses should be cut.

Tigereye: A golden striated form of Quartz which glints with a form of chatoyency and is opaque. A naturally lucky stone, Tigereye was thought to stimulate and clarify the thoughts of its wearer.

Smoky Quartz: A tan to dark brown type of transparent Quartz, sometimes incorrectly called

Smoky Topaz. It was thought to be lucky for foresters and gardeners.

Rutilated Quartz: Clear Quartz with golden needles of rutile crystals scattered throughout the stone.

Tourmilated Quartz: Clear Quartz with black tourmaline crystal needles inside.

Quartz crystal points are quite popular among New Age believers and are thought to focus the spirit's inherent power toward healing and self improvement. Rutilated and Tourmilated Quartz are thought to be especially good receptors and amplifiers of ethereal energies.

Rock Crystal balls are the traditional crystal ball and were used as tools to divine the future and commune with the spirits.

Hardness: 7
Toughness: Good

Quartz has long been associated with the crystal ball.

Ladies' Tourmaline and Diamond ring: 14 Karat Gold.

Ruby

Ruby's name comes from the Latin root word "Ruber" meaning red, from which also is taken the name rubellite for red tourmaline. It is the red form of the gem corundum and is second in hardness only to diamond. Occasionally rubies occur with minute inclusions arranged in a pattern which reflects a floating six rayed star when viewed under a single light source. These are known, appropriately enough, as Star Rubies.

Rubies are found in Thailand, Burma, Kampuchea, Kenya, and several other countries, often in alluvial deposits where they washed down rivers as gravel and collected in pockets of gem gravels.

Burmese Rubies have always been thought to be the finest and most celebrated. The king of Burma was called "The Lord of the Rubies." The stone was sometimes known as Oriental Ruby, to differentiate it from lesser stones. The Burmese believed that Ruby ripened in the ground, starting as yellow and changing and deepening until it achieved the vibrant crimson color.

There are many properties tied to this renowned gemstone. Because of Ruby's blood red color, its magical significance is often tied to curing diseases of the blood and stopping bleeding. Tales are told of warriors who had rubies implanted under the skin to bring valor in battle. It was rumored to light darkened rooms with its glow and boil liquids when placed within them.

Ruby was supposed to ensure harmonious physical and mental health, bring peace, and guard homes and fields against storm and catastrophe. The fiery red gemstone was said to attract and maintain love, and ward off sorrow, inspire boldness and bring success in business.

It was supposed to keep away plague, and relieve pain. Ruby would warn its owner against disaster by turning black when danger was near. As an interesting parallel to physical reality, Ruby will turn black when heated with a torch, returning to red as it cools.

Eastern legends said that Ruby adorned the heads of dragons, and could not be damaged by fire. It was believed to be a charm against evil and ward off dire thoughts.

In the Hindu religion, Ruby is ranked first among gemstones. It is said to be the highest offering to Krishna.

Hardness: 9
Toughness: excellent
Birthstone: July

Sapphire

When the mineral corundum is red in color, it is known as Ruby, but the name Sapphire applies to any other color. So, other than color, Ruby shares Sapphire's physical characteristics and vice versa. The most well-known color is blue, but Sapphires are also beautiful in shades of pink, yellow, and other colors. The most desirable color, if blue, is said to be cornflower blue - an intense color, neither too light nor too dark. Sapphire's name was originally linked to the color blue, and some of the legends surrounding the stone might actually apply to other blue stones such as Lapis Lazuli.

Sapphires are found mostly in Sri Lanka, Thailand, Australia, western USA, and Tanzania. Historical sources include Burma, and the Kashmir region of India. As with Rubies, they occur sometimes as star stones where a six rayed star shimmers within the stone.

To some religions the blue color represents the heavens. Blue Sapphire has been a holy stone to the Catholic church, and to ancient Persians, who believed that Sapphire made the sky blue. It was identified with chastity, piety, and repentance, and it is said that King Solomon wore a Sapphire ring. Sapphire would keep one's thoughts pure and heavenly and help those in the right find justice in legal matters.

The Gemstone was also thought to be a powerful amulet to protect against poisons and cure ulcers. The Sapphire warded off poisonous creatures, and killed snakes hiding nearby. It would also cool fevers, sharpen eyesight, and protect against mental illness.

The most important attribute of Sapphire was said to be that of protection against sorcery. It was thought to banish evil spirits and frighten devils. It would turn evil sorcery and negative spells back against the sender, provide advance warning of hidden dangers, and free the mind of the enchanted.

Sapphire was important to wizards and seers who used it to help interpret visions and prophesies. It was thought to be effective in quelling inflammation of the eyes.

Hardness: 9
Toughness: Excellent
Birthstone: September

Tanzanite

A rich blue-violet gemstone, Tanzanite was discovered in Tanzania in 1967 by a prospector looking for sapphire. The prospector, Manuel d'Souza, originally from India, had been looking for stones in the wilds of Tanzania when some natives took him to an area about 60 miles southwest of Arusha. He soon discovered the blue stones he had found were not Sapphire, but staked a claim and began mining anyway. Henry Platt of Tiffany and Co. named the new gem "Tanzanite" and Tiffany's began a marketing campaign to introduce it to the public.

It remains a popular stone for all types of jewelry, and is still only found in quantity in Tanzania. In nature, Tanzanite only sometimes occurs as a blue stone, but more often is golden to brown. It is a variety of the mineral Zoisite. It was discovered that by heating the brown or golden variety of the stone and gradually cooling it, the color could be permanently changed to the violet-blue color.

Tanzanite is pleochroic, which means that the blue and violet tones vary depending on the angle the stone is viewed from. A variety of Zoisite is sometimes called chrome Tanzanite, owing to its green color caused by chromium.

Tanzanite is too recently discovered to have any magical properties attributed to it.

Hardness: 6-7
Toughness: Fair to poor, avoid rough handling

Topaz

An island in the Red Sea, known in antiquity as Topazion, probably the modern island of Zeberget, gave Topaz it's name. The stone was at one time predominantly found there, but now the major sources are Brazil, Nigeria, Australia, Burma, and Mexico.

True Topaz is found in shades of colorless to yellow, orange, red or brown, and is sometimes treated by irradiation to produce blue colors. The term Imperial Topaz refers to stones with a fine peachy to reddish orange color. It should not be confused with Citrine or Smoky Quartz, both of which are sometimes erroneously called Topaz.

The old traditions hold that Topaz bestowed many benefits upon its wearer. It would relieve bad dreams, dispel cowardice, calm the temper, cure madness and plague, and sharpen the wit. It was thought to aid in sleep and eliminate nightmares, as well as cure rheumatism and soreness in the joints. Topaz was also credited with being effective against bleeding and heart disease. The gem was said to instantly lose its color to indicate that poison was present, thus protecting its owner.

Topaz was also thought to bring fidelity and friendship if constantly worn without being set aside. It was also believed to be an effective talisman against accident and fire, and to bring increased intuition and long life.

To Christians, Topaz has been known as a symbol of uprightness and virtue.

Hindus believe that worn as a pendant, this gemstone will relieve thirst, sharpen intelligence and lengthen one's life. It is thought to be the ideal stone for travelers, protecting them from accidents and homesickness.

The ancient Romans credited Topaz with preventing sickness of the chest and abdominal tract.

Hardness: 8
Toughness: Poor to fair
Birthstone: November

Tourmaline

The gem Tourmaline gets its name from the ancient Sinhalese word "Turmali" which means multi- colored gems. This is because Tourmaline occurs in virtually every color of the spectrum. Some examples even have multiple colors within the same stone, the result of changing conditions during its formation. The most popular colors of Tourmaline are green, red, and pink.

Although mentioned as far back as Pliny's Natural History in the first century (it was then called Lychnis) Tourmaline has often been the victim of misidentification. Finds of green Tourmaline brought back from the New World were sold in Europe as "Brazilian Emerald" until the realization that it had a property known as pyroelectricity. Pyroelectricity is a legitimate 'magical' property. When gently heated, Tourmaline generates a static electrical charge which attracts dust and other lightweight objects.

Because of its vivid colors and relatively affordable cost, this gemstone is a popular choice for fine jewelry of all kinds. It is found mostly in Brazil and Afghanistan, but also in the USA, Burma, and India. Some names given to tourmaline's colors include:

Chrome Tourmaline: An intense, often dark green owing to the presence of chromium in the stone.

Indicolite: From the word Indigo, a deep blue to blue-green color.

Rubellite: Pink to deep red, from the Latin root work "Rub" for red.

Watermelon Tourmaline: A stone which shows pink and green together, often with a yellow divider. Most properly this should be a slice of a Tourmaline crystal that shows red surrounded by a green 'rind.'

Tourmaline was thought to be an aid to meditation, fostering compassion and cool headedness. It was said to protect its wearer against many dangers, particularly that of falling. The gem was highly valued by alchemists who, possibly because of it's pyroelectric effect, believed it to be related to the philosopher's stone. This was said to be the substance that would grant enlightenment, give power over spiritual affairs, reconcile opposites, and change base metals to Gold.

Hardness: 7-7.5

Toughness: Fair

Birthstone: October (along with opal)

Ladie's Tourmaline Ring.

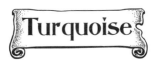

Turquoise

Mention Turquoise, and most people will probably think of Native American silver jewelry set with the sky blue gemstone. Turquoise has always been highly venerated in Native American traditions. It is an essential presence in the Shaman's medicine bag. It can be a simple nugget or bead, or it may be carved in the shape of a totem animal, and adorned with feathers and bits of stone tied to it with sinew. The Pueblo people often placed Turquoise in the floors of their dwellings to bring good fortune. Although Turquoise is closely identified with Native Americans, its lore and appreciation stretch across the globe.

It was discovered by the ancient Egyptians around 3000 BC and was used widely in their finest jewelry and ornaments often combined with Lapis Lazuli and Carnelian as in the treasures of Tutankhamun's tomb. The Turquoise was carved into scarabs, and representations of the various gods and worn by the priests for ceremonial purposes. The ceramic Faience was developed by the Egyptians as an imitation for Turquoise and Lapis Lazuli.

Old European traditions associate Turquoise with horses, and hold that the stone will protect horses from all sorts of ills. In particular, it was said to prevent them from drinking overly cold water while overheated and foundering. Turquoise was said to enable its wearer to resist evil and maintain virtue. It was credited with helping achieve a state of higher consciousness and resistance to weakness. It was also thought to protect its wearer from falling, particularly from towers and horses.

Tibetans revere the stone and believe it represents good fortune, good health, and that it provides powerful protection against the evil eye. Turquoise is used in Tibetan healing ceremonies, where a Turquoise bead is thought to hold the shadow soul and draw out illness from the body. Buddhists associate Turquoise with knowledge of the future.

Many Tibetans still wear necklaces with Turquoise, and coral beads which are hundreds of years old, and Turquoise often adorns ceremonial objects. In both Tibet and Nepal, Turquoise is highly esteemed and can also serve as currency.

Today the major sources of Turquoise are Arizona, plus Australia, Chile, China, and Mexico. The stone often occurs with veins of matrix which add interest to its beauty. Body oils can sometimes cause Turquoise to turn green with time.

Hardness: 5-6
Toughness: Fair to good
Alternate birthstone for December

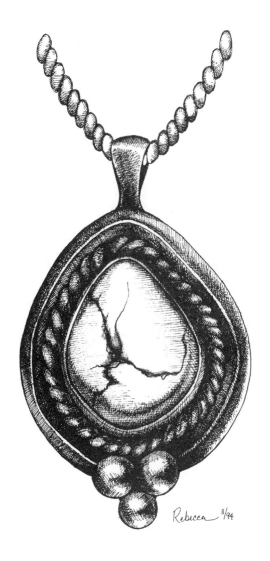

Turquoise has long been a favorite in Native American Jewelry.

Man's Lapis Lazuli Ring.

Zircon

A brilliant gemstone that occurs in several colors, such as green, yellow to golden tones, and brown. Many brown Zircons are heated to enhance their color to shades of greenish blue ranging from light colors to vibrant blues. The name Zircon may have come from the Persian word Zargun, meaning gold colored. The stone has been known variously as jacinth or hyacinth and as jargoon. Today we simply call it Zircon, usually preceded by its color name, such as blue Zircon or yellow Zircon.

In Europe's medieval times, Zircon was believed to bring wealth to its owner, cure insomnia, bestow honor and wisdom, and to keep away sickness and evil spirits.

Found in Sri Lanka, Kampuchea, and Burma, Zircon is prized by Hindus who ascribe to it the power to remove fear, clarify the mind, and induce spiritual growth. Their astrologers say that the Zircon should be purchased and set by the jeweler on a Saturday of an ascending moon.

The genuine gemstone Zircon should not be confused with cubic zirconia, a man-made imitation for Diamond, or with synthetic Zircons used to simulate other stones.

Hardness: 6-7.5
Toughness: poor to good
Birthstone: December

Other Gemstones

There are hundreds of species of gemstones ranging from the familiar to the most rare and obscure. While they cannot all be allotted feature pages in this book, there are a few more worth mentioning.

Amber

As the fossilized sap of primordial trees, Amber sometimes features entrapped insects or bits of leaves. It is found primarily in the Dominican Republic and along the Baltic coast of eastern Europe.

Hardness: 2-2.5
Toughness: poor

Andalusite

Andalusite is a transparent gem originally found in Andalusia, Spain but now also in Brazil and Sri Lanka. Dichroic, or multi-colored, it shows different colors when viewed in different directions, usually orange and green. Related variety chiastolite shows a cross pattern and is opaque.

Hardness: 7-7.5
Toughness: Fair to good
Sometimes substituted for Alexandrite as June's Birthstone.

Coral

Coral is formed by tiny sea creatures as a external skeleton and home for their colony. Porous, but often shiny, its most valuable color is red. Coral also occurs in pink, white and salmon colors and in black, gold and blue. It is prized in Italy and the Himmalayas for its talismanic effects.

Hardness: 3-4
Toughness: Poor to Fair

Kunzite

A relatively recent discovery, Kunzite is named for George Frederick Kunz, who in the late 1800s was a pioneer of gemological science. This rare gemstone displays a delicate light pink to lavender color. This color will fade over time if exposed to strong sunlight and care should be taken to protect the stone from sharp blows or scratches.

Hardness: 6.5-7
Toughness: poor

Spinel

A transparent gem that occurs in colors of red, pink, orange, blue, violet, and purple. Found in Burma, Sri Lanka, Thailand, Kampuchea, and the USSR among the same gem gravels as Ruby and Sapphire. Up until about the mid-1800s this stone was not known as a separate stone, but was confused with other gems such as Ruby.

Hardness: 8
Toughness: Good

Appendix

The Birthstones

January: Garnet

February: Amethyst

March: Aquamarine

April: Diamond

May: Emerald

June: Pearl and
Alexandrite

July: Ruby

August: Peridot

September: Sapphire

October: Opal or
Pink Tourmaline

November: Topaz

December: Blue Zircon

Anniversary Gemstone List

1 — Gold jewelry
2 — Garnet
3 — Pearls
4 — Blue Topaz
5 — Sapphire
6 — Amethyst
7 — Onyx
8 — Tourmaline
9 — Lapis Lazuli
10 — Diamond jewelry
11 — Turquoise
12 — Jade
13 — Citrine
14 — Opal
15 — Ruby
16 — Peridot

17 — Watches
18 — Cat's eye
19 — Aquamarine
20 — Emerald
21 — Iolite
22 — Spinel (all colors)
23 — Imperial Topaz
24 — Tanzanite
25 — Silver jubilee
30 — Pearl jubilee
35 — Emerald
40 — Ruby
45 — Sapphire
50 — Golden jubilee
55 — Alexandrite
60 — Diamond jubilee

Glossary

Asterism - the phenomenon Which appears as a star floating in a gemstone. It is caused by minute inclusions arranged along the crystal planes of a gemstones form.

Brilliance - white reflections and flashes of light reflected from within a gemstone.

Cabochon - a rounded or domed - top polished stone, without facets.

Carat - a unit of weight for gemstones, originally derived from the weight of the carob seed. Today 5 carats = 1 gram.

Chatoyency - a phenomenon similar to asterism, but in which a single line, similar to a feline eye appears.

Crystal - a mineral form which has an orderly arrangement of atoms often with a specific shape, and bounded by plane like faces.

Cryptocrystalline Aggregate - a stone formed from many tiny crystals linked together to form one mass.

Cultured Pearl - a pearl formed by the insertion of a nucleus, around which the oyster creates a pearl.

Dichroism - the property of a gem that is transparent and transmits two different colors when viewed in different directions.

Dispersion - the separation of light into different colors.

Double Refraction - the separation of light into two separate rays as it passes through a stone.

Enhancement - a process which improves a natural gemstone.

Facet - a small flat polished surface of a gemstone. A stone that has many facets is said to be faceted.

Freshwater Pearl - pearl type found in a freshwater mollusk.

Inclusion - an irregularity which can be seen in a gemstone, by the naked eye or with magnification.

Karat -a measurement of the pure gold content of a gold alloy item. expressed as 1/24th of pure gold, the rest of the content being other metals.

Lustre - the amount of light reflected by the surface of a gemstone.

Mabe' Pearl - a pearl which occurs as part of the shell of a mollusk. It is therefore flat on one side, where it was cut from the shell.

Mother of Pearl - a term for the polished, lustrous, but flat shells of some mollusks.

Nacre - the substance an oyster deposits in order to form a pearl.

Natural Pearl - a pearl which forms by an accident of nature within a mollusk.

Orient - Iridescent sheen on some pearls, in which light is broken up into several colors.

Overtone - a secondary color superimposed over the body color of a pearl.

Piezoelectricity - the property of a material generating a static electrical charge when compressed.

Pyroelectricity - the property of a material generating an electrical charge when heated.

Play of color - a brilliant display of multiple colors caused by the prismatic effect of an opal.

Pleochroism - the property of some transparent gems in which different colors can be seen when the stone is viewed in different directions.

Potch - opal lacking in play of color.

Rough - an uncut, unpolished gemstone.

Translucent - an object which transmits light, but through which objects may not be clearly seen.

Transparent - an object which passes light through itself with out distortion.

Sources

Biedermann, Hans, Dictionary of Symbolism
New York; Penguin Books USA, Inc; 1994

Black, J. Anderson, A History of Jewelry
London, Orbis Publishing Limited, 1981

Bratley, George H., The Power of Gems and Charms
California, Newcastle Publishing Co. Inc, 1988

Bruton, Eric, F.G.A., Diamonds; Second Edition
Pennsylvania, Chilton Book Co., 1970

Cavey, Christopher, Gems and Jewels, Fact and Fable
New Jersey, Wellfleet Books, 1992

Cunningham, Scott, Cunningham's Encyclopedia of
Crystal, Gem and Metal Magic
Minnesota, Llewellyn Publications, 1993

Dickinson, Joan Younger, The Book of Pearls
New York, Crown Publishers, Inc, 1968

Druxman, Barry, A Jewelers Guide to Gemology
Washington, NGI Publishing Co., 1986

Ghosn, M.T., Origin of Birthstones and Stone Legends
California, Inglewood Lapidary, 1984

Healy, John F., Pliny the Elder's Natural History, a selection
New York, Penguin Books USA, Inc; 1991

Johari, Harish, The Healing Power of Gemstones in Tantra, Ayurveda, and Astrology
Vermont, Destiny Books, 1988

Kozminski, Isidore, The Magic and Science of Jewels and Stones, Vol. 1 & 2
California, Cassandra Press, 1988

Kraus, Edward Henry and Slawson, Chester Baker, Gems and Gem Materials
New York, McGraw-Hill Book Company, Inc, 1947

Kunz, George Frederick, The Curious Lore of Precious Stones
New York, Dover Publications, 1913

Newman, Arnold, An Illustrated Dictionary of Jewelry
New York, Thames and Hudson, Inc, 1981